Plainsongs

Editor

Eric R. Tucker

Associate Editors

Becky Faber, Michael Catherwood, Eleanor Reeds

Editors Emeriti

Dwight Marsh, Laura Marvel-Wunderlich

Publisher

Corpus Callosum Press

Cover art by Chris Goedert

Corpus Callosum Press
Hastings, Nebraska

Subscriptions to *Plainsongs* are $25.00 annually for two issues, published in January and July.

Plainsongs welcomes submissions. Contributors will receive one free copy of the issue in which their poem appears. For each issue, the Board of Readers will select three poems to be honored as award poems. Award poem winners will receive a small monetary amount, currently $50.

Please use our online submission manager, available at the Corpus Callosum Press website, to submit work. Though we will endeavor to consider all e-mailed and snail-mailed submissions, we cannot guarantee responses for work submitted via these methods. Non-submission-related correspondence can be e-mailed to etucker@corpuscallosumpress.com or mailed to Corpus Callosum Press, PO Box 1563, Hastings, NE 68902. For more information about submitting poetry or subscribing to *Plainsongs*, please see our website: https://www.corpuscallosumpress.com/plainsongs.

Cover art by Chris Goedert.

Plainsongs is indexed by Humanities International Complete, EBSCO Information Services, 10 Estes Street, Ipswich, MA 01938.

ISBN-13   979-8-9853780-4-7

ISSN 1534-3820

Plainsongs

Winner of the Jane Geske Award,
presented by the Nebraska Center for the Book

Notes from the Editor

Thank you for picking up the winter 2023 edition of *Plainsongs*. As always, we are grateful for your readership. This issue features award-winning work by Michael Phillips, Natalie Marino, and Katharina Mohr, whose poems are accompanied by essays written by our dedicated trio of associate editors/poets/scholars/all-around wonderful humans, Becky Faber, Michael Catherwood, and Eleanor Reeds. Continue flipping pages and you will discover eighty-three additional poems by poets from across the United States and around the world: a treasure trove of powerful, evocative, thought-provoking pieces to fire up your neurons and feed your winter-weary soul.

Plainsongs is now in its forty-third year of continuous publication: a noteworthy feat in a publishing marketplace that has not been kind to small, niche literary journals. Its longevity is due in large part to the efforts of former editors Dwight Marsh and Laura Marvel-Wunderlich, who worked so hard for so long to keep this journal alive and healthy, and to the long-standing commitment and patience of the associate editors. *Plainsongs* got its start in 1980 at Peru State College in Peru, Nebraska, and spent the vast majority of its life (from 1983 to 2020) at Hastings College in Hastings, Nebraska. Fittingly, it will return to HC following the release of the spring/summer 2023 issue, which will be my last. It has been such an honor to be the editor of *Plainsongs* for the past eight years, and I am very excited to see what the future holds for this spunky little journal.

On the evening of Saturday, April 1, 2023, Corpus Callosum Press and Hastings College Press will cohost an evening of poetry and prose readings at the Lark in downtown Hastings to kick off National Poetry Month and to celebrate forty-three years of *Plainsongs* and its imminent return to Hastings College. This will be our first in-person poetry event since the start of the pandemic all those eons ago. If you happen to find yourself in south-central Nebraska on that weekend, please come by the Lark to say hello and take in some terrific live poetry. We'd love to see you there.

Thank you for your support of *Plainsongs* during my time as editor. We wish you all the best in 2023 and beyond.

Eric R. Tucker
Hastings, Nebraska

Contents

Burning Leaves 10
    Michael Phillips
About "Burning Leaves": A Plainsongs Award Poem 11
    Becky Faber
Letter to a Young Woman Poet 12
    Natalie Marino
About "Letter to a Young Woman Poet":
A Plainsongs Award Poem 13
    Michael Catherwood
A Man in a Podcast Tells Me How to Speak 14
    Katharina Mohr
About "A Man in a Podcast Tells Me How to Speak":
A Plainsongs Award Poem 15
    Eleanor Reeds
neon 16
    Lyndsey Kelly Weiner
Sea Glass 17
    Briana Craig
Break me 18
    Peter Shaver
Fallout 20
    Jack Granath
Boundary 21
    Matthew J. Spireng
Ripeness 22
    Frederick Pollack
Empty Playground 23
    Dana Stamps, II.
Epistle of a Physics Laureate 24
    Alan Elyshevitz
Collecting Dandelions 25
    Yvette A. Schnoeker-Shorb
Vacancy 26
    Ken Autrey
A Note for Ophelia 27
    Stuart Stromin
Latchkey Kids 28
    William Miller
Bones 29
    Ellen June Wright
The Emerald 30
    Naomi Dean
Upstairs windows. 31
    DS Maolalai
Daughterless 32
    Beth Suter

Children's Hospital 33
    Max Heinegg
Windshield Time 34
    L. Sweeney
It's Animal 36
    Jill Burkey
The Apron 38
    Stelios Mormoris
It's All Right 40
    Eunhee Soh
Domine, Deus 41
    Libby Maxey
On Seeing a Mirage at a Vons Parking Lot 42
    Isabella Cruz Pantoja
Envoys 43
    Zoe Boyer
I hold my chest, too 44
    Sonia Aggarwal
In my house, with bones showing 45
    Duncan Richardson
Not a Sonnet on Not Being in Love 46
    Laura Gregory
Lighthouse 47
    Stephanie McConnell
a poem is a bit like a bench 48
    Remy Chartier
Barren Corn Fields 49
    Deidra Suwanee Dees
Intermission 50
    Grace Kwan
I could learn from him 51
    Thomas DeFreitas
Untitled 52
    Callie S. Blackstone
The Janitor and His Wife 53
    Danny Barbare
Aubade with Love 54
    Gospel Chinedu
How to Read a Poem 55
    Christine Pennylegion
Dear Grief 56
    Susan Michele Coronel
Museum of the Modern Horror Film 57
    Kathleen Madrid
The Summer of Starting Over 58
    Laura Walker
Side by Side 59
    Donna Pucciani
Les Giboulees de Mars 60
    Sara Epstein

The Estuary 61
    Julia Dallaway
Reunion 62
    Rebecca Yancey
"Sorry, We're Closed For Good" 63
    Robert Fillman
My Mother's House...64
    Stellasue Lee
A Poem About Not Coming Out 66
    Hallie Carton
Moving On Up 68
    Jude Atwood
Nameless Cove 69
    Ruth Holzer
Pain Level 70
    Renee Emerson
The Magician's Conquest..71
    Amanda Tumminaro
Jello in Hard Times: Cranberry-Apple Salad 72
    Dawn Terpstra
creatures are longer and more blind 73
    Josie Levin
the west coast is on fire & 74
    Shilpa Kamat
We Have No Obligations but Us Tonight...75
    Z. Unger Bell
denouement 76
    Grace Rea
I Never Climbed a Tree 78
    Rodney Torreson
Sugar Mountain 79
    David Stephenson
just a few steps more..80
    Haley Sielinski
Returning to the Village 81
    Stephanie Niu
Saffron Walden..82
    William Heath
Ode to the sprig of rosemary 83
    Cassady O'Reilly-Hahn
Moonlight Is an Icy Fanfare...84
    David M. Alper
Kettling...85
    Tim Kahl
The Same Is Always Now...86
    Michael Salcman
Red-winged Blackbirds...87
    Jennifer Fandel
Solitaire 88
    Deborah Pope

Sebastian to His Wounds 89
    Lee Rossi
Ode To Dawn & The Coffee Jug 90
    Olumide Manuel
The Land of Not Enough 91
    Paula Reed Nancarrow
Pomegranate Seeds 92
    Katey Linskey
Last Day in Kinsale 93
    George Looney
Among the Dying 94
    Devon Balwit
Snow Day 95
    Joanne Esser
Idyll for a Barn Collapsing 96
    Frank Coons
Let It Snow, Let It Snow, Let It Snow 97
    Joseph Stefani
Ode to Roadkill 98
    Zachary Rea
Train 99
    Micah Daniel McCrotty
Situation Comedy 100
    Ruth Towne
Barn Swallow 101
    Amanda Smith-Hatch
Parking Lot Present 102
    Susan Wolbarst
Synchronicity 103
    Cathy Porter
How to Dream in Russian 104
    Katy Fitzpatrick Shedlock
Jazz 106
    Becky Kennedy

Burning Leaves

We burned leaves back then—
late November most years,
when the township gave notice
of a day with no rain or wind forecast.
My dad sprinkled kerosene and lit the match.
My brother readied the hose, just in case.
With steel rakes we turned the pile over,
folding and churning, feeding the flames,
bandanas covering mouth and nose.
Up and down the block, neighbors did the same.
Columns of smoke rose singly from yards
and converged over town to blot the sun.
Smoke penetrated wool and flannel,
settled on our skin and hair,
and clung to the back of the throat.
Smoldering leaves crackled and crumbled.
Hot ash sifted down through the pile,
carving a wound into the lawn spring would heal.

Michael Phillips
Chadds Ford, Pennsylvania

About "Burning Leaves": A Plainsongs Award Poem

My October trips across Nebraska have included magnificent views of leaves in brilliant fall colors. As I drove, Robert Frost's poem of 100 years ago popped into my mind: "Nothing Gold Can Stay."

"Burning Leaves" beautifully continues this thought. It begins as if it were the re-telling of an ancient practice "back then," conducted at a certain time after official notification was given.

A reader might anticipate that a poem about fall leaves would include a reference to deciduous trees, but there is none. Instead, the focus is on the process of burning leaves, laid out for us step-by-step. For those of us who have experienced this ritual, it brings back memories; for those who have not, it suggests a physical process. The poet has added initial steps—"My dad sprinkled kerosene and lit the match / My brother readied the hose, just in case"—as well as the work of handling the pile of leaves, "folding and churning, feeding the flames."

Two aspects of this poem stand out as particularly skilled writing. One is the detailed olfactory aspect: "Smoke penetrated wool and flannel, / settled on our skin and hair, / and clung to the back of the throat."

The second is the use of effective verbs for movement of action. How better to describe the leaves in the pile other than that they "crackled and crumbled"? This leads to the "Hot ash sifted down…, / carving a wound into the lawn…."

The lines are tight and clear. What a wonderful tribute to this beautiful season!!

Becky Faber
Lincoln, Nebraska

Letter to a Young Woman Poet

Write before your voice is gone,
before the last door closes. Write
a sonnet for your mother.

Let the world know she held
your face to her chest on nights
you were afraid of the dark.

Write about love
and sweat on Sundays.

Write the delight of nursing
in the blue
of early morning.

Write an ode to your daughters.

Show them even on joyful days
life is hard,

that you choose to continue
showing up, that you know you are
a parachute.

Write a lyric with light
falling from the late afternoon sky,
with the music of rivers.

Forget the critics.

Write how spring tastes
like lavender.

Write an elegy to dying leaves
so you can remember
the sound of time as it burns.

Natalie Marino
Thousand Oaks, California

About "Letter to a Young Woman Poet": A Plainsongs Award Poem

The epistolary poem has a long and deep tradition in literature. It can capture both wisdom and compassion. Natalie Marino's "Letter to a Young Woman Poet" is a brilliant poem that shifts and pauses and drills deep with its honesty and strength, engaging the reader with both a conversational voice and a lyrical tone.

The poem employs direct advice while employing repetition of the word "Write." Marino begins, "Write before your voice is gone, / before the last door closes." Marino creates a poem of love and instruction, holding both complexities at once, a gentle balance that builds both authenticity and sincerity. No small achievement. The speaker's pronouncements about a mother provide force in the poem, an attribute the speaker wants to emphasize for the "Young Woman Poet":

> Let the world know she held
> your face to her chest on nights
> you were afraid of the dark.

The speaker also mentions challenges: "Show them even on joyful days / life is hard…" then she adds white space for emphasis, "that you choose to continue / showing up." The line break at "continue" holds the reader and maintains a duality of not only "showing up" but also living on.

Later, the speaker demands, "Forget the critics." This straightforward guidance mingles with wonderful imagery:

> Write a lyric with light
> falling from the late afternoon sky,
> with the music of rivers.

The focus on the mother and daughters connects the reader to the "Poet." There's a strength in the voice, advice the speaker has earned, and we know this voice, the voice that persists, that chooses its path, that does not allow the poet's voice to be tamped down. A poet's voice is the poet's gold, the breath that poems require, and the breath the poet requires.

Michael Catherwood
Omaha, Nebraska

A Man in a Podcast Tells Me How to Speak

From my sister's throat flower
carnations; stalks bladed by lips,
syllables bleeding against street
lights & neon hospital ceilings.

A girl walks into the E.R. (midnight),
a girl walks into a bar (moonlight),
a girl walks into *just-a-joke* (carnations

slice her lips, bleed roots into her lungs;
fluorescent blooms, broken ribs: a map of
tendons inside her flesh, cut vocal, cut fry.
A nurse strips over/ripe vowels from grating
chords, rips petals from her velum) (a girl)

(walks into) (E.R.) (silence); the nurse drowns
consonants in radiopaque exclamation marks
(question mark). The girl suffocates on contrast
medium, *contrast* meaning men with language,
medium meaning cut your body open, split your
bones, drown in white blood cells; let his voice
cut questions, cut marks, cut chords, cut pitch,
cut *like*, cut *believe*, cut carnations; cut also: girl.

Katharina Mohr
Paderborn, Germany

About "A Man in a Podcast Tells Me How to Speak": A Plainsongs Award Poem

Katharina Mohr's title invokes a self-inflicted experience of mansplaining that is not explicitly described until the final lines in which the speaker lists the feminized markers of speech to be "cut…cut…cut…cut" as this imperative itself becomes a verbal tic. Rhetorical violence is always already embodied violence in this poem as *"just-a-joke"* concludes a series of parallel traps into which a "girl" may walk that begins rather than ends with the Emergency Room. This clinical setting with its "neon…ceilings" features medical personnel whose speech is "radiopaque," an evocative neologism that indicates the density of both Mohr's descriptive technique and sonic effects throughout "A Man in a Podcast Tells Me How to Speak."

The central visual metaphor of the carnations, flowers as much associated with the artifice of hospital florists as with the organic—if invasive—growth later suggested by "roots" and "blooms," demonstrates the shifting applications of such an image. While initially the "stalks" are "bladed by lips," we then learn across a stanza break that "carnations // slice her lips" as the sister's body is shown to be less of a weapon and more of a target. By the last and longest stanza, the disintegration of this body has accelerated as Mohr's introduction of the second person inflicts "men with language" who "split your / bones" upon the reader too.

The visual and aural elements of this poem persistently function in tandem: for example, "strips" becomes "rips" in a sonic echo and a vertical alignment. One can imagine "A Man in a Podcast Tells Me How to Speak" being performed with striking viciousness because of its staccato rhythm and plosive effects and yet, without the text itself, a reader would lose the complex rhetorical cues provided by Mohr's use of punctuation, especially parentheses. This is a poem of accumulation and abruptness that I find, even in these brief reflections, so difficult to disarticulate as I endeavor to account for my sense of its profundity and brilliance. This very impossibility of paraphrase is the highest compliment I can offer Mohr as she transforms the Romantic consumptive into that figure of modern tragedy, the cancerous.

Eleanor Reeds
Hastings, Nebraska

neon

my house & my neighbor's house
log cabins at the end of a packed-dirt road
meant to be sisters

last night he hung a *bud light* sign in his window
it flashed over the chickens roosting on the porch
on   off   on   off

I sit on the stone tile next to my son's bath
knitting around & around a sock meant for his father
we haven't seen him in a year

through the fogged window the snow flashes
bent tubes of noble gas casting their blue beacon
over the frozen pond

Lyndsey Kelly Weiner
Erieville, New York

Sea Glass

Scars don't heal, they have already healed.
They are the mark of the healing, the afterthought,
the impression of a moment, sung by the finest
calligraphy voices of a thousand fibroblasts.
Today, I dedicate an orchestra to those who have
made sheet music out of skin.

The mother of the sea will rub salt into our
wounds until the edges become soft and round.
I write her hymnals and pray every broken bottle
gets polished in the waves. That the shores
will sing in technicolor, and we will walk
on the sands of what was once sharp.
We will collect the tunes of our shattered
souls and display them in a glass jar
above the piano, where our inner child
practices her chords in the morning.

Do you see how the dawn light makes them glow?
Can you hear how miraculous this music is?

Briana Craig
Rockville, Maryland

Break me

I have to work my faith like a muscle.

I imagine being swallowed by the world,
struggling in a small green cavity
and holding to my recollections.

Poison ivy grows under a fence
and my nephew gets a blister.
Would it be a lie to tell him it'll get better?
I pray he'll live to know worse.

A sweet old woman
who survived the Depression,
a bastard of a husband and son,
gets edema in her legs.
With help you can live well
under the confinements of age.

It always confuses me when someone asks
who decides who suffers?
It'll come to everyone.
We all hear a siren howl,
see children and old folks huddled at the store.

With will,
some things we can
stop.
Some things no one deserves.
The best is hard enough.

Suffering is in the core.
You can say there is no meaning in it.
But there is.

Smell the cool night wind.
A woman has been shot in the back by a stranger.
Who will protect her
and change the man
who did this?

Break his heart so that he sees.
Break me.
Let me see.

Peter Shaver
Shavertown, Pennsylvania

Fallout

La lluvia ya no me conoce.

The day sound, muffled now, seems alien,
But which one is the stranger here, this thing
Or me? It makes a difference—still a kid
In far too many ways, I know the sense
Of having all my senses jammed against
The old official story of the world,
But now, this spring of the pandemic blitz,
It feels as if the ripples are reversed:
The blushing sunlight finds me strange, the wind
Darts anxiously in its attempt to lose me,
While redbuds bend their fresh, young limbs like dancers,
Who would, if clumsily approached, shy off
And laugh together, covering their faces.
The cold clouds mass and turn their backs on me,
Creating shadows in the peonies
That loll their heavy heads. The rain begins,
A gorgeous, condescending summer shower—
The rain, it doesn't know me anymore.

Jack Granath
Shawnee, Kansas

Boundary

Between two fields, fallow now, what
would be a hedgerow, were there hedges,
but instead there is low brush—elderberry
and blackcaps, pokeweed and young mulberry

blooming or bearing fruit other times of year—
among big trees—black cherry and soft maple—
a trace of old barbed wire and a few stones
lugged from the fields, a patch of nettles

on the edge one place, milkweed another,
and a hole here and there with soil mounded
around where woodchucks have made their
homes between one man's field and another's.

Matthew J. Spireng
Kingston, New York

Ripeness

It's possible that failure ends.
But you have to become it in time.
Too early, and youthful hormones
sour into rage;
too late, and heart lungs liver punish you.
Do it right and you find yourself,
as Marx said, proletarianized,
though without his promised change in consciousness:
your triumph a walk to the drugstore,
successful eradication
of mold from a shower curtain,
each meal, each check you can cover.
And the world you inherit
will be white strips of cloud
reinforcing sturdy grey,
like an advanced cardboard.

Frederick Pollack
Washington, D.C.

Empty Playground

    Cracked, grass growing through it—a white
plastic bag caught in weeds—
        the pavement surrenders.

    Newspapers scrape across asphalt
like tumbleweeds, and jet
        engines are rude sirens in the smoggy sky.

    As dandelions and daisies dab
        yellow, a cur pees
on a rusty shopping cart next to a discarded condom.

    During some summer, long ago, a jump rope
thwacked the hot
        ground, and little feet stomped

during hopscotch. Now, kicking
        debris aside,
    hair raises like fire on the back of the neck.

Dana Stamps, II.
Riverside, California

Epistle of a Physics Laureate

Gentlemen, The fruit cup is an analog of isotropic
and homogeneous space in that cantaloupe, pears,
and grapes taste identical in added sugar. And yet

I hunger at every point in the visible universe.
Third-generation quarks trouble me—as beauty
is troubling, as truth is an ongoing quest. I have sent

this letter in my stead, remote as I am in a rented tuxedo.
What does it mean to give the bride away like the neutron
gives itself to decay? Hand on hand, the newlyweds

slice cake while I consider branes and how forces leak.
Years ago, during Feynman's lecture on bicycle pumps,
the air came out of parenthood for me. It was the knowledge

that even mesons could sire and dissolve. So who
was I in my macroscopic virility? I stare at a flotsam
of fat cut away on a catered plate, relax into aphasia

and the glittering music of a wedding band, the slavish guests
commanded to dance, mimicking quantum states. At the final
ceremony, I dodge the multiverse of a tossed bouquet:

one blossom the playground of my first sprained wrist,
another the housefire of my sister's sobs, the last a petite
dimension restraining my mother's nerves, my father's gravity.

Alan Elyshevitz
East Norriton, Pennsylvania

Collecting Dandelions

The antiviral activity of dandelion extracts indicates that ... components of these extracts possess anti-influenza virus properties.
    —from an article on the NIH website

Way too many people
are dying—and, yes,
I take it personally, yet
dandelions, yellow bursts,
flourish forth, break through
cracks in cement, in asphalt,
in anything seemingly
impenetrable—hope
as a metaphor, field guides
for survival; my mask
boasts their printed patterns,
contains what remains
of my dignity; I didn't ask
for a spring full of rain
and viruses, droplets
windborne, worldwide.
Outside vitals—blood
pressure, glucose, oxygen—
there are lives unmonitored,
breathing, pulsing, flowering,
fluffy, little floral puffs,
each new morning enough
and every day ideal,
full of expectation.

Yvette A. Schnoeker-Shorb
Prescott, Arizona

Vacancy

In the house my father built,
his power reaches through
light sockets, shivers up
from air vents, scuffs the floors.
He's left behind his tools,
down to the teeth of his saw,
the drill bits, shoe polish, keys.
Here he is in the bookshelves
and the lock on the bedroom door.

When my daughters come
with their children, where do they
find me, now that I'm alive?
In this house, my father's house,
their father's house, those are
my fingerprints on the door.
They wonder where to find
an open room, a spare
place at the table.

Ken Autrey
Auburn, Alabama

A Note for Ophelia

To make
my quietus
would be *loverly,*
to end the daily terrors
of riding the random wheel of fortune,
like a man astride
the stripes of a pet tiger.

It doesn't take much.

And yet,
no matter
which way the wheel may spin,
as history will testify,
there can be many winners.
Roll on up!

To sleep,
dream on, drift away on drowsy lullabies,
float on the ephemeral tranquility,
like ripples across an endless lake,

like feathery stalks of dandelions wafting on the wind.

It doesn't take much.
It takes barely a blade.

It makes hardly a splash.

And yet,
while we live and breathe,
the grim sergeant of death will be upon us soon enough.
There are precious drops of time to savor.
And—where I rest—
of course,
There is your life,
       there is your life,
              there is your life.

Stuart Stromin
Los Angeles, California

Latchkey Kids

Summer in south Florida, no air except for giant fans
that spread more hot than cool—I taught drama
to seven poor children.

I was poor, my first teaching job, three an hour,
no rulers, no paper or scissors, Elmer's timeless glue.
We twisted fairy tales into odd,

funny, shapes. They acted out "The Three bears"
as robots; Goldi was a spoiled brat who took what
she wanted since getting what she wanted

was all she knew. This little girl, the smallest,
played a passed-out bear and said all the bears
should be passed out drunk like her parents

in front of the tv. Too funny, too real, my parents
did the same, their friends, strangers, crashed
out among empty beer bottles,

greasy paper plates. I had to step over bodies
to get to the back door while the sun came
up slowly, the only light I could depend on.

My boss said the parents would be offended
on "Parents Night," refused to let them perform.
I spoke up, even cursed, was fired

on the concrete spot. I left without a word,
like parents leave and never said goodbye.
But they had seven names, faces, seven different

stories of neglect. Latchkey kids we were and still are,
wait for a grown up to come home, tell us when
to go to bed, turn out the light.

William Miller
New Orleans, Louisiana

Bones

You knew nothing of Hamlet or Yorick
of court jesters or men longing for their fathers,

but wondered if these unfleshed bones
washed clean by the sea, bleached by the sun

belonged to white man or black man.
The dead are dead, bones are bones

fit only for casting spells, for divination
for placing into a leather pouch hanging

on the wall to ward off evil spirits—
to show there are already ancestors here.

Ellen June Wright
Hackensack, New Jersey

The Emerald

Northern slip of the country, western
edge of a time zone, dusk swoops in
late, like our curfew. Neon blinks on,
greasy and sugar-laced, at Mouth Trap
Cheese Curds and Sweet Martha's Cookies.

We've earned a respite from stretches
of soybeans. Smushed-together fairgoers
spill 1919 root beer to our delight.
We catch the sparkle of dairy royalty,
Princess Kay of the Milky Way, crowned
and carved in butter as we wait for
malts too thick for their straws.

The emerald of a building lights our
way home, columns reaching up
and back to the WPA, my grandma
baking bread to show off and hope.

We've exhibited all that we can:
rhubarb jam, stringy and beckoning;
ewes, aching for birth; bread we call
our own; songs, upbeat and longing.

We've captured all that we can:
falling out of ourselves at the top
of the ferris wheel, purple ribbons
on 4-H exhibit cards, breathing
with hundreds of girls in triple decker
bunkbeds, too full of the fair to sleep.
We'll keep it with us, for our lives
remaining, ordinary except for this.

Naomi Dean
Plymouth, Minnesota

Upstairs windows.

bar windows light nights
like an ember in long-dying
fires. I am walking—I am not
walking anywhere.
just walking—I walk
to get out and see night
coming down like a hood
on a thick-skin wool coat.
I love it as wordsworth
loved to see daffodils—to look up

sometimes and to see
upstairs windows,
in this bedsit-lit cityside
neighbourhood, move. smithfield
has life in it—not
just a "nightlife",
but people who live
here as well. people who go

out to bars and who don't.
like opening cupboards
and finding six-month-old potatoes,
their eyes become long
purple stalks. outside
of the bars, people smoking
and talking a little. the cricket-
sound sparking of lighters around.

DS Maolalai
Dublin, Ireland

Daughterless

It doesn't matter to the oak
where its acorns get buried by jays—

what does it mean to you?
Mythical girl, I never knew you

my scratched hands full of blackberries
grandma Phoebe rinsed in the creek.

She didn't have a name for what drew her to the woods
though she prayed, feeding winter cardinals

bright as *love-lies-bleeding*—
my mother's language of flowers—

ovaries blooming like water lilies
a zygote rooting, or not, in the blood forest.

I wish I could give more to you
than what I've seen of winged creatures.

When your mother doesn't know, who are you?

My first word may be my last: *Phoebe*.
Perched above the dark waters of the lake

drunk on grandpa's wine from wild pears
I watch the wind on yellow daisies

and you, always you,
keeping me company among the hard woods.

Beth Suter
Davis, California

Children's Hospital

—May 2020

The princess is bedecked in sweat,
the wires flow out of walls.
Blood flecks her gown by her left arm,
the heart monitor frogs.

Sandpaper gasps outside the door,
a gaunt boy on a gurney.
Her room's small clock, its tiny sink,
child-sized ceremonies.

Outside, the night deliberates,
reprieve is all I ask.
The morning nurse arrives to read
the verdict to us, masked.

Max Heinegg
Medford, Massachusetts

Windshield Time

Thrust into the dusk I have no map no GPS no plan
other than to arrive in Lake Charles stay at the hotel

we stayed at in May. Alone. Crammed into my Camry,
beef jerky, seltzer water, and dog beside me, I'm

preoccupied by our road trip south, then in sunny spirits,
except for pulling over at the casino where you

racked up credit card bills which you could never pay
even via eBay selling. Still, you were good

at stopping at farmer's markets for jam and honey,
pausing at the gourmet place sampling cinnamon & sugar

glazed pecans in Missouri. I pull over, sleep somewhere
in Kansas. In the morning head towards Joplin then Mena,

that classic car place, remember our daycations in your Chevy,
how you revved your engine when a sports car threatened.

When I get to Shreveport, exhausted, it is night and
I'm no good. I stay at an overpriced hotel. In the morning

second guess myself. Instead of heading south towards
the village where we noshed on shrimp and hush puppies

I turn north toward Colquitt, call my counselor. Not long after
leaving Lake Charles, you said *I feel like your lackey.* We bickered

at a roadside stand where you plucked a wildflower for me,
bickered at the rest stop where you clapped your hands

mocked my feisty streak, bickered at night in the hotel room's
bathroom though you held me close, but I didn't sleep.

By the time we made it north into Amish Country, you kissed me.
Somehow, I turn south again though I don't take the route

to that village where we picnicked. I remember our last night
in Lake Charles at Chastain's Food & Spirits seafood restaurant.

We talked about the poets, a trio of pixies, and I apologized
for getting on your nerves about directions, though you

guided this Iowegian through Cajun country. When I arrive
in Lake Charles, I pull over at the same hotel where we stayed

in May. At Rikenjaks, I order a beer and burger, remember
the night you asked if I was staying. You cooked crock pot,

your famous chili, I read poetry about the U.P., your home state.
We made out in the hallway, listening to *Across the Universe*

and then your snoring. I wonder what you are doing, what
kind of stories you're telling, spooked out of your mind

about me relocating or quitting our enterprise, but what the heck
I said, we could weather it, we'd made it this far hadn't we.

Despite the recession. In the morning I rent a garage apartment
in the historic district where you heard an electrical spark,

that's rare you said.

L. Sweeney
Bloomington, Illinois

It's Animal

"It's animal" is a line from Ellen Bass's poem, "After My Daughter's Wedding."

The only outward sign my daughter is nervous
on her first day of 9th grade is her t-shirt that says
Being Brave Can Change the World.
She smiles while I click her picture—
ponytail, ripped jeans, silver Birkenstocks.
My husband and I hug her tight, lingering slightly,
then watch her stride alone up the street to her stop.

When her bus drives by the house,
I wave a little wave.
She waves a little wave back.
Not much else is little anymore.

I carry my coffee to the back patio
where I sit with the crickets and our beagle,
who has helped us see her off since first grade.
My hand reaches down to find the comfort
of her soft, familiar fur.

Crickets chirp. Doves sigh.
The silent scent of honeysuckle.
A plane flies overhead.
A bird I can't name ventures into the silence
with a melancholy sound the shape
of an unanswered question,
the slow sound of sublime longing.
Plates clink as my husband empties
the dishwasher inside.
The sun softly continues to rise.

I spy my son's elbow through his window
as he zips open his bedroom blinds.
I'm a hummingbird hovering around the edges of his life,
flitting between bits of nectar he sometimes provides.
Cherry tomatoes thrive on the vine
like the symphony crescendoing from his speakers
in perfect succulent pops.

When it's time, we follow him to the driveway
to see him off on his last first day of high school.
He barely waits for me to snap a photo—
sunglasses hooked in shirt collar,
mala twined around his left wrist.
With his tuba in the back
and trombone in the trunk,
his car is a shrine of instruments,
his head is full of plans.
So much ripe in this world.

We wave as he backs down the driveway,
smile as he lurches into first,
still learning the clutch and roll of the manual.
We stare down the empty street
long after he has disappeared,
then climb the steps to the silent house.

I thought my first-day-of-school emotions had subsided;
that as the kids had grown, I had too,
but tears arrive as I try to apply mascara
and again while I'm driving to work.

I remember our old cows at the ranch—
their ragged hides and wise, calm eyes.
No matter how many calves they'd had; eight, nine, eleven,
they still mooed frantically at weaning time,
still paced the gate with spry, young steps,
ears pricked forward, tails swishing,
pausing every now and then to paw the ground
and moo mournfully over the fence,
their entire body heaving sound across the empty pasture.
Silence the only response.

I always wondered why they didn't give up sooner.
Now I know:
It's animal,
this love.

Jill Burkey
Grand Junction, Colorado

The Apron

I am wearing my mother's
apron I found on the inside
of the cupboard door
aged to a peppery beige.
The shock of it hanging
on a nail, slump-shouldered,
as if she had just slipped out

in a rush to die as she was
making stewed lamb and
greasy potatoes and crispy
phyllo rudders through me.
She likely left the candles
burning on the perfectly
set table, tines of forks
glinting like the tiny knots

of silver crosses sewn
into the bishop's robe
that would one day cordon
her rose-sprinkled grave.
Now at her seat at the head
of the table preside shakers
of rice coupled like dolls,
and bowls of rubber grapes.

I tie the belt loop around
my broadening waist, filling
out her form to prepare
the meal she never finished.
I pat down the crumpled
lap of shorn linen, marked
by raised red embroidery
of the word 'Mom' in script.

Cheap sentiment, yes,
but I ride a passing longing
feeling the soft edge

of the page she thumbed
as I decipher a recipe for
lemon soup she wrote in
pencil, smudged to a sheen,
marred by a few dry stains.

Ironic how this apron covers
as it cloaked me once before:
the summer of 1957 over
the flow of steaming casseroles
and sisters' muted screams
to cheers of ballgames
and activists for civil rights
in the blistering TV set

as she carried me inside her
through the battered rooms
whose wounds I grew to love—
as I set this plate of hot rice
to swinging bells of incense,
Kyrie Eleison, three times—
to the timer clicking shut.

Stelios Mormoris
Boston, Massachusetts

It's All Right

There was no connection
between the two distant trees
in my backyard until I found tiny
white seeds captured in air, languishing.
The glints of breeze revealed the silvery string's ends—
how did a slight spider link the two trees.
It must've flowed from one to another,
swimming in the pool of sunlight
to survive against gravity.
The cottony seeds hung patiently
like a language
while my friends' deaf son played under the trees,
pulling rocks, lifting his eager face,
then reaching out to me
soundlessly
it's, all, right,
it's, all, right.

Eunhee Soh
Pleasanton, California

Domine, Deus

My friend and my neighbor you have put away from me, and darkness is my only companion.
   —Psalm 88:18

We neighbors, each a troubled house packed tight
with all the stuff of living, saw her coming,
attic spilling more of grievance than
the street could hold. What luxury to shut
our doors. The children told her all their news.
She brought them dollar treasures, popsicles;
they left her letters without stamps. Somehow
we, torpid under August, didn't notice
when the law descended. But they took
her house; she took her cancer and was gone
to where—we asked each other—no one knew.
As if the place of exile were a street
address. To which abyss? Which cast-off pit?
Which is the country where all is forgotten?

Libby Maxey
Conway, Massachusetts

On Seeing a Mirage at a Vons Parking Lot

It must have been the midday sun which lent
a phantasmagorical sheen to the pavement
that day.
And the pavement must have been wet or
humid or naturally perspiring at least like
everyone else that morning since it hadn't
rained the night before, not a single drop,

but multiple somethings were taking shape
regardless, were climbing up onto
themselves and growing sinuous and lively
right before our eyes looking like us and yet
not like us
faces in dimmed lights
their strange angular features inching closer
and higher

and then farther

and smaller

as we stood there
eating olives straight out of the jar
fishing them out with our fingers as children
would and plopping them into our mouths
the brine on our tongues almost like
the brine of the not-ocean on the ground and
the not-ocean on the horizon and
the real ocean,
somewhere beyond that lot
becoming more restless by the minute,
and bridging the distance.

Blinking away the mist,
this staring continued.

Eyes as wide as sinkholes.

Isabella Cruz Pantoja
São Paulo, Brazil

Envoys

Slivers of wild carrot
fall away from the knife in rounds,
fat coins gleaming dully in the kitchen light.
A sweet, vegetal scent wafts from the cut flesh
sparking thoughts of the world outside—
fecund spring soil and nascent buds unfolding
in origami whorls—sights I have yet to see,
sequestered in this season of pandemic.

But for now it is enough
to be chopping these carrots,
inhaling the dampness of distant earth where,
though I can't see them, I can still wonder
at taproots snaking beneath the loam,
cells swelling to golden spears, a lacework
of emerald leaves unfurling overground,
gathering sunlight for the shade-bound
to savor with their morning meal.

Zoe Boyer
Prescott, Arizona

I hold my chest, too

when I can't seem to take it
all in, don't see how I fit
into all of this. This house
was never mine. But its ghosts still
stroke my hair at night,
bend their knees on my floor
and tell me
I've lost something. A child
sits on a boat, crushes a pistachio,
and spoons kulfi in her
grandmother's mouth, too cold
for more. They move
closer, huddle under a stole
and listen to the waterfall
while the child's mother takes
a picture.
        It's still there,
wrapped in tissue, inside the envelope
with the same ten-dollar bill
my Nani would keep
for a rainy day, sitting on the second shelf
of her old, scuffed dresser in Delhi.
I need to go get it.
It must still smell of her pearl soap
and incense, and have a crease
down the center from where she would rest
her thumb as she so often did
with her prayer books. But I can't. I can't
go back.
        This house isn't mine. I hold
my chest tighter and the skin reddens.
This life can never be mine. I live
in a house with nothing
but ghosts still stroking my hair
every night.

Sonia Aggarwal
Reading, Massachusetts

In my house, with bones showing

1
the dark wood soaks up light
in the late afternoon
mellow and strong
drying out
after just another flood

staring back
the surprise at this meeting
        all mine
finding room rib shadows
the frame of a ghost door
lost footfalls of a place
fused with my skin

2
skeletons make us look small
human or house

so hurry
pull on your flesh

and let us soon return
to peel away

this silence

Duncan Richardson
Corinda, Australia

Not a Sonnet on Not Being in Love

He falls head over heels in love each time.
"I had the biggest crush on…" so-and-so
Who later broke his heart. By contrast I'm
Too cautious. Not a risk-taker. I know
"'Tis better to have loved and lost." I know
I've never "dared love anyone that much."
Thanks Tennyson. Thanks *Good Will Hunting*. So
My inexperience has been my crutch
But I'm too old for ingénue-ity.
I am afraid. Ashamed. Impatient. Dull.
I'm hashtag blessed with ingenuity
And charm, thick eyelashes, a sturdy skull—
Plenty of XP for this quest called Love.
If I were badass, independent, brave—
Like a "real" feminist—I'd rise above
My fear, stride forth, and grab love by the balls.
But I'm no warrior. I'm passive and
I like my cozy white archaic tow'r.
So, metaphorical cliché in hand,
I wait and work and pray I don't go sour.

Laura Gregory
Grand Island, Nebraska

Lighthouse

I miss you less here where
the Atlantic smacks so like a lover
the rocky shore. Leaving, I thought
the longing to be wrapped inside you
like a storm, to be devoured by you
like a field does a seed or coin
would linger, follow. Take
to the road and track me down.

I do miss how good
being tired with you
felt. And the way you felt.
No one else will ever
pronounce words how you do.

The light whirls back and again
in the dark. It is far-reaching, but
steady. They called those who
first came here *keepers*, despite
all they had abandoned to arrive.

Stephanie McConnell
Norwood, Massachusetts

a poem is a bit like a bench

started in middle school // not touched again until you've finished your BA // still messy // slopped over with too much shellac // *you never really learned the trade* // decorated with ~ ~ ~ // and mahogany // you love the word-color mahogany // deep red-brown elegant soil // stained on the surface // *you remember the drafts underneath* // unpolished // (it looks more authentic that way) // (what is authentic) // (why does rough-raw mean authentic) // *this is not the kind of art you thought you'd be making* // *not the kind of art you studied* // hands cramping // all those splinters // so afraid // terrified of the carving // shearing out chunks to discard // lost scraps littered across the cutting room floor // unrecognizable // sucking on your finger to stop the dripping // (the red-brown dripping) //
   pricked
on the tip of your tool

Remy Chartier (they/them)
Daly City, California

Barren Corn Fields

barren corn
        fields

that I picked
    in childhood

give way to
thick   emerald green

    forests

that hold
my

minivan on the road

as I   drive
from the rez to campus

to teach
    Cultural Studies

Deidra Suwanee Dees
Atmore, Alabama

Intermission

Double bass reclined
sidelong in the spotlight,
neck bared—
steel tendons belie tender rust. Whose
fingers are so lucky as to smell
of oxidized metal tonight? Light glimmers
off a maple shoulder, but before I can think
it begs for a kiss she hauls herself upright
moseys offstage and I follow. Into the wings,
arms of spruce whispering against me,
hardwood sinking to loam underfoot, then
sand. Looking around I shout
her name but the sea air snatches it
from my mouth, gives it
to the tide and I haven't finished
speaking I want to be worth her
manipulation I walk with my body bent
against wind even though there is none then I see the shape
and colour of her
approaching along blue shoreline
feet submerged in overturned sand face tilted
toward mine hand staying imaginary wind
from blowing the sweater off
that shoulder and my
relief aches a symphony.
The first violin draws breath.
The buffeting wind sounds
like a wrung A-string.

Grace Kwan
Vancouver, British Columbia

I could learn from him

His handsome poem
ambles down the page
in workboots, khakis,
and a corduroy vest.

Doesn't need rhyme
any more than a lilac
needs cologne, or Jesus
needs televangelists.

Might be having a
bad day. Shrugs it off,
and gets on with the
business at hand.

Thomas DeFreitas
Arlington, Massachusetts

The photograph captures him
leaning back in the chair, stretched out
from the tips of his 70s hair to the toes
of the decrepit bowling shoes.

The man who steals her from you
hides his face from view, his profile obscured,
the golden outline of glasses prominent
over the dated flannel we all thought was hip.

The keyboard waits in front of him, waits
for him to put it in warp factor 5, waits
for him to type out the love letter
to the girl you are still fucking,
the midwestern girl who only knew rows and rows
of corn before the east coast. Now she knows
the smell of salt. He will whisk her out of your apartment,
he will steal her away to that city of steel.
He will pour pickle-backs down her throat after
the vows, he will announce the baby by making a hip
movie reference. Warp factor 5, yeah,
warp factor 5.

He'll steal your girl.
Warp factor 5.

Callie S. Blackstone
Connecticut

The Janitor and His Wife

Says the janitor
I sweep to hear her
whisper
like a wind across
a golden field.
And I am a willing
ear.
And I mop to
learn how to
dance with her.
And we just have
fun
as if to let it
all wring out
like a bucket of
water.
That is why I work.

Danny Barbare
Greenville, South Carolina

Aubade with Love

& we choose to split—our hands,
memorizing the alphabets of love
but from right to left. memories:
mortals that crave resurrection even
before death. i want to be a long
story, not told in sentences. every
word holding its breath till the end.
& if you die telling my story, it
means, i was never really important.
& if you live, it means, i'm in-
complete & there's something you
left unsaid. let me start here: i'm in
no hurry to stop writing about love.
what i cannot contain is the reflection
of every moment bright in the dark
of my eyes. i lick the last letter of your
name & my tongue glories in the
hunger. this way, i keep a part of you
intact. an icicle hurting my favourite
tooth. a temper rising in my mouth.
a tempest, in the offing. now do you
see that a closed mouth is the nearest
thing to resistance? & sometimes,
silence keeps us from peril. i dye my
tongue with a bird's blood. suddenly,
my mouth lathers with white songs.

Gospel Chinedu
Ozubulu, Nigeria

How to Read a Poem

First hold it in your hand a while; just sit
and feel its weight. Note how the sun glints off
each burnished face. Now feel along the sides
until you find the lock: so small it seems
no key could fit inside. It's only love,
as straight and slender as a pin, that will
unlock its heart. Lift up the lid. Beneath
its mirrored surface living clockwork ticks
and carries every word from thought to heart
and back again. Keep watch until you know
its inner secrets better than your own.

Or: stick a nail right through the lock, force thumbs
through crumpling walls and pull the halves apart
like rotting fruit. You can reduce it all
to sad component parts: a pile of screws
and rusting springs and cogs with broken teeth.
There's always one that's somehow missing when
you try and fail to make it whole again.

Christine Pennylegion
Windsor, Ontario, Canada

Dear Grief

You're so thirsty for the past
that you make your own prayers
but to me they sound like hornets,

rainbow glass in my gut,
the crunch of gravel underfoot
where only sad wives walk.

The whitewashed walls know you,
sense the thinning blood of time.
You're unquenchable, not for water

but for bone dry wine. Face to face
with you, I'm a coward in a clown suit
who recalls the lapsed chord,

the bare belly, the capsized coin.
Why do you triumph when my outsides
are pushed in, my insides

positioned further away from life's joys—
mint, the lull of babies' laughter,
ridiculous stars? You put your finger

on the egg in the sky because it's fractured.
I want to be washed into lightness
but all I can do is sense gravity

slip, wonder at the aching silver
of what's lost, the frayed summer,
fish teeth persistent in the dark.

Susan Michele Coronel
Ridgewood, New York

Museum of the Modern Horror Film

About teenage sex, and suffering, they were not wrong,
those movies of the 1980's. How
girls missing their fathers were easy, pleasing

    prey for monsters.

        I hated those Final
Girls the ones who didn't
need like

    I did. How I wanted

to be the one who was too
loved

    to be eaten.

Kathleen Madrid
Centennial, Colorado

The Summer of Starting Over

The sun never set while the deer carcass rotted away. It was near the end
of a summer, the bones of my heart [b]leached in the suddenness of desert.

We the living can only see death in melodrama—slow-motion impact, rent
flesh; then comes the collapse, the final breath into animal lungs. We see dust

eddy. We know nothing of endings really, only what's left behind: the hovering
stink, the fly clouds, the death grimace widening into a smile. An invitation.

Laura Walker
Cedar City, Utah

Side by Side

Unfathomable how piles of stones
that separate farmer's fields can hold them together,
crisscrossing Britain, shoulder to shoulder
and shoulder high, without a lick of mortar,
sheltering a pasture full of wide-eyed sheep,
their wool wet with mist and wonder.

Nothing glues the rocks together
but morning dew, their angular, awkward shapes
leaning into each other for balance,
keeping the flocks from straying on the road,
where bikers threaten or trucks loaded
with fragrant hay could kill.

Seen from afar, tipsy trapezoids of granite
tumble down the meadows, swerving
around the bends and rills. A public footpath
leads through a snicket, where the stone wall
uncoils serpentine around a hill full of lambs.
Sprays of heather and moss surprise dark boulders

humped between buttercups, and forget-me-nots
sprinkle the sun among the crevices. There, a daisy
dares to wave among the ivy, where the wall
runs past the village pub to pray church-side,
preaching its own sermon on serenity,
and bells ring out the interconnectivity of shapes.

Donna Pucciani
Wheaton, Illinois

Les Giboulees de Mars

Rain! Our constant companion on this visit to my niece in Paris.
She tells us the new phrase she has learned:
"Les giboulees de mars."
We repeat after her,
skipping as she does over the middle vowels,
as we shop for a new raincoat for my sister:
"Les gibblay de mars."

I try to remember the phrase
by telling myself it sounds
like the splatter of rain on the street,
on my umbrella,
on my daughter's hair
as she refuses to walk underneath the umbrella with me.

My sister finds a chic brown coat,
which suits her style and her dark hair,
and I try out the phrase with the salesgirl,
who emphasizes the "OU" sound in the middle.

Paris is ahead of us, a month ahead—
the dictionary defines the new phrase as "April showers"
but it is the middle of March,
and magnolia trees are blooming,
willow trees are leafing.

The next day we sit in the restaurant at Musee D'Orsay,
frowning at the glare of the unfamiliar sun
that drowns out the pastel beauty
of the fresco painting on the ceiling.
When the sun goes behind clouds
and rain returns, we see gold and flowers
shine instead inside the room.

Later, in Sainte-Chappelle chapel,
we hear a string quartet play Vivaldi,
punctuated by the drumming of rain on the ancient roof.

Sara Epstein
Winchester, Massachusetts

The Estuary

Our mothers took us out
    as far as the estuary, gave us a taste
        for the salted breeze.

In our knotted hearts, we felt
the rival tugs of generations:
our mothers' fear of the uncharted, our daughters'
        unborn ghosts longing to be free.

One hour with you, and the brackish water
        opens out into the wild sea.

Busied by the child in the crook of her elbow,
neither of our mothers saw her homely cottage
        from this great distance.

It is given us
to re-shape the lineage,
to honour and to counter their self-sacrifice
        with our own
            imperceptible gifts.

Julia Dallaway
Oxford, United Kingdom

Reunion

Eating chicken salad
under the flapping tent
with forks clattering,
napkins blowing,
I heard the announcement:
you had been killed, buried
In an unmarked grave.

At first I could remember
nothing of our time together.
Were we friends? Lovers?
Did we study together,
heads bent to our books?
Did we run for the classroom,
dripping from the rain?
Did we quarrel?

Then I remembered:

In the town square late at night
we were sitting under a tree,
your head in my lap.
The grass was moist.
Your lips were dry.
We felt no need for talk.

Rebecca Yancey
Lebanon, Tennessee

"Sorry, We're Closed For Good"

—for the folks at the Alpine Downtown Eatery

We drove through the night, checked in
to a cheap motel, didn't

sleep. Up early and hungry
we walked into town, where we

found a family diner,
the lights on. We had our pick

of empty booths, sat ourselves,
made small talk with the owner.

His teenage daughter brought eggs
and black pepper, extra toast.

She topped our coffees more than
necessary, gave a small

wink when she slipped us the bill.
Of course the prices were good.

The girl at the register,
a slightly younger daughter,

smiled when we paid. The whole place
was bright and clean. We made sure

to mention it. How shiny
the counters were. We told them

we'd be back again next year.
We weren't just saying that.

Robert Fillman
Macungie, Pennsylvania

My Mother's House

A naked man is passed out in the living room.
I find Mother in her bedroom, naked,
grinding her teeth. Both of them,
sleeping it off.

This isn't just a lucky guess;
the kitchen is full of empties.
The weather has been dreadful,
mold cultures on dishes.

The dog follows me
happy for some company.
I shove clothes off a chair
and sit looking at the man.

He isn't bad looking, really—
he's young—very thin.
I try not to stare at his genitals,
but rather at the fine sheen that covers

his body. The dog lifts my hand with his nose—
what a life the poor beast has.
The house smells of sweat, dog,
and old dead soldiers.

I get up and fill the dog's bowl
with fresh, cool water.
The humidity today is 90%.
If I leave now,

neither of them need know
I was here.
There's enough trouble
between Mother and me.

From the direction of the bedroom,
I hear the sound of a toilet flush.
God, this is the hottest damn day.
I don't see it cooling off soon.

Stellasue Lee
Knoxville, Tennessee

A Poem About Not Coming Out

I don't tell people I'm queer.
Instead, I tell them,
"I went to see Lucy Dacus in concert and cried during 'Christine'."
Instead, I cuff my jeans and dye my hair blue.
Instead, I make eye contact
                when I tell someone I like their septum piercing.
Instead, I read poems about women
during the open mic at the independent bookstore. Instead, my
    Picrew profile picture
              has pink, purple, and blue stripes in the
                  background.
Instead, I quote Judith Butler.
Instead, I cared
    deeply
        about Kurt and Santana from Glee
when I was in middle school.
        Instead,
I stopped going to church.
Instead, I track hate crime statistics and restrictive legislation.
Instead, I look over my shoulder when I hold a girl's hand in public.
Instead, when my job at the textbook publishing company says
we have to change a passage where a boy wears nail polish,
I scream into my pillow at night.
Instead, instead, instead
I do not come out.
I reject the idea that straight is the default and queer requires
    declaration;
that hetero is the norm but queer is framed like an apology,
with parents who,
    if you're lucky,
        say they love you *anyways*,
as if you have done something wrong
and have been graced with forgiveness.
I do not want grace.
Instead, I want indifference.
Instead, I want to blend into the crowd.
Instead, I want to take a girl to the park,
a blanket shared beneath us,

weaving flowers together
for her silk soft hair,
and to plant a kiss before I place the crown.

I want everyone in the world to know what I am,
and for them to never care at all.

Hallie Carton
Boston, Massachusetts

Moving On Up

When God closes a door, he opens a window.
Rob him.
Steal his blender and the good towels.
The fancy ones—in the upstairs bathroom, not the half-bath near
 the kitchen.
The blender with blades so fast it can make hot primordial soup.
And Egyptian cotton towels made from real Egypt.
Don't fold them, roll them, like that lesbian couple showed you in
 Mammoth.
Show them off to guests.
"So soft!" they'll say.
"They used to be God's," you'll confide,
"But now they're mine."

Jude Atwood
Costa Mesa, California

Nameless Cove

The winters are bleak, the land flat,
just a few scraggly windswept trees

and rocks scattered all over.
If I moved there, the total souls

would still number under a hundred.
I'd live in a white clapboard house,

drive a pickup truck, have a boat,
maybe a dog. Clear a garden plot

for turnips and cabbages.
I'd lock up my trash

from the scavenging gulls.
I'd see wandering icebergs,

sometimes the Northern Lights,
and across the Strait, the coast of Labrador.

At the liquor store I'd meet my neighbors,
Dempsters, Walshes, Diamonds,

who never have much
to say for themselves either.

Ruth Holzer
Herndon, Virginia

Pain Level

I wish I'd left the bloodstains
on her swaddle blankets.

They came out so easily, as easy as
the smell of her—
morphine, wire, nurses' gloved hands.

Like a child running
away, down the hospital hall I swung
the bag of soiled belongings,
returned with powder soft rolls of muslin.

A white flag, a shroud,
a Jesus robe, a baptism.

Her heels could fit between
my finger and thumb, crosshatched
from the needles interrogation.

Is this her normal work
of breathing?

The chest dips in, catches
the cry from her mouth—
a butterfly—settling now
in my own throat.

Renee Emerson
St. Charles, Missouri

The Magician's Conquest

Although I was the girl in the magician's box,
sawed in half, and fading to the air,
my heart is still green with envy.

I heard you've a new lover, pulled from a hat,
awing the audience with clap and stare:
A show of carrot and rabbits mating.

I've attempted to sew myself into a new doll,
but with no luck, no luck at all:
This is my cue to bid adieu.

You've juggled my heart, my mind, my soul,
with, I must say, some small success:
Ruining my reason, a triple threat.

I long to erase you, but it's not as simple as that.
Your circus, it seems, is always in town.
My cot lies you down to sleep.

But come one day, there will not be so much ado,
much ado about a big red nose and big shoe.
It's fair to say I have bid you adieu.

From the cage of my zoo, I bid you adieu.

Amanda Tumminaro
Dixon, Illinois

Jello in Hard Times: Cranberry-Apple Salad

Cherry gelatin tendered with ground apples & walnuts
From her orchard, cranberries from the grocers she traded
For fresh cream & eggs collected on double-overcoat dawns.

She whips the skimmed cream, crowning jewel-colored
Gel in pink Depression glass. The bowl rises like a
Baptismal font from a lace-covered table, laden with

Mashed potatoes, glazed ham, cookies & mincemeat pie.
The blooming Christmas cactus casts a shadow, roots older
Than Mother, longer than Great Grandfather's sacred promise,

Leaving them for bottle and boarding house after the Spanish
Flu. Once a year a meal unites and redeems family. Hands
& food—blessed, old & new trespasses—forgiven. As heads

Bow she prays before spooning redemption onto old
China—the taste of Christmas melting on the tongue.

Dawn Terpstra
Lynnville, Iowa

creatures are longer and more blind

creatures are longer and more blind
the deeper you find them. It's about
necessity. Eyes are meant to fail.
Itch, pink, pitch. There are tools for this.
You can find them in the sand. Sharp
between the grains. A zebra mussel
isn't near as exotic as it sounds.
It's home: on the arch between the ball
and heel

The beaches in Wisconsin are not
significantly colder. it's the people actually.
They turn somewhere in the middle
of the lake. Next to one of the tankers
no longer looking forward but back; if you've
got a grandmother she's wary of the riptide.
And your ankles. If you don't. Well.
There are newspaper clippings, too.

Less can see you in the lake
than on land. If you're past the buoys,
what comes to the surface
are tourists. Without your glasses
everything is a particularly quick wave.
Blotting your blush on its gills.
It's much too soon in meeting
that you feel each other. too smooth.
Two different kinds of teeth.
It's an embrace. Or rapture.
Neither of you know
what the other can live without.

Josie Levin
Wheeling, Illinois

the west coast is on fire &

moments before evacuating california
       for vermont two of the children wonder
              why they have never seen baby mermaids

& I suggest that mermaids lay eggs
       but nurse their babies

                     & the girls laugh
in consent before joining the hug line

& then the family drives away   leaving
       clothes & scissors   rice & toothbrushes
              memories of unseen/untasted mermaid milk

as they text from the haze of their journey
       across Utah   Nebraska   I wonder
              If the kids will spot mermaids evacuating the smoke

carrying their eggs from estuaries holding
       saltwater tanks as they swim upstream   or
              perhaps they must guard their eggs in bays

microscopic ash making them nauseous even
       underwater like we are even through double
panes   smoked in   waiting for ocean winds

Shilpa Kamat
Richmond, California

We Have No Obligations but Us Tonight

and so I'll leave the window cracked open
because I know you love the smell of rain
and *petrichor*, you'd call it
petrichor with hands wrapped around a mug,
burn scar of your right palm against the handle,
you never did learn to wait
singed your tongue every time
even after stirring in cold milk.
I leave a quilt
over the back of the sofa
so you can reach for it
when you sit in the recliner
and you don't have to pull awkwardly
from behind you, arms twisting
while I build a fire.
Home, they say, is a hearth.
A heart lit aflame and burning
gently with intensity and
I don't know who *they* are
but they certainly got it right,
petrichor in the kitchen
and heat in the living room
burning through the chill of the wandering wind
meeting your eyes and begging
a god I never believed in
god let me light these matches
for the rest of my life

Z. Unger Bell
Hamilton, Virginia

denouement

      hunker down honey
         look to the dogs
            them can scent a plot
               from any yard
            know when to retreat
         under the porch
follow the bones

      it's daughters
         who keep secrets
   code messages
      in clapping games
         wedge rocks
         in window frames
       forward the action   write notes
   love and suicide

so maybe I left you

   a low path through smoke
   a vase of my breaths

      I want us to meet at the epitaph
   I want
   a technical descent
      with well-made ropes
         not the hot sparking
        bash
        of stones

but I've raised a rottweiler in my throat

      all I can do is shout
        the way
     down

sensing the hound moon
    the sun also
        barks madly

Grace Rea
Cranbury, New Jersey

I Never Climbed a Tree

except for one with its high limbs low
and then would climb down
the combination branches, my mouth
and hands purple with mulberries, never clambering
for climbing's sake, but admired taut
arms and legs required for taking command,
ascending the sloping boughs
with poise and balance to keep going
shin to shin on a tree's trapeze.
When a young poet stalled, I'd tell them
they might write about climbing a tree.
Maybe they did. But the yes kids
would get only a little higher than the ones
whose smiles would chafe at the notion,
until finally it happened, after I retired.
I sat across a restaurant booth from a teenage
girl with flashing blue eyes and ribbons
of laughter, one wrist feasting on bracelets
and under the table long legs that looked like
they could hold a table up, and calves
with bundled muscles, which made it look
like she could really go—a green but leafy
young poet—who'd already made it
into *Rattle* and the *Louisville Review*.
In no time she was up and scaling,
she and the wind both angling, matching
the hurtling of the knobby branches,
scrambling up every which way and me admiring
a brilliant girl who had branched
into other fields too. I didn't know,
but it was the last time she'd write for me,
as up where the wind was leaf-smacked
she scaled, way up and out the top of her poem.

Rodney Torreson
Grand Rapids, Michigan

Sugar Mountain

Some ants have broken through my kitchen screen
and follow a zigzagging formic path
across unnatural terrain to reach
the sugar bowl, their world's new center-point.

I wonder if they have mythology
explaining it, with ur-ants and whatnot;
if so, I have a prophecy for them
about a scowling, vengeful, bug-spray god—

or I could fix the screen or move the bowl,
avoiding the Old Testament approach.
They're only following their destiny,
like humans, cashing in on a windfall,

and I am wary of inviting Death
onto my property, lest he decide
to bag an extra target while he's here.
So I will fix the screen, and think of them

back in their anthill, telling wide-eyed tales
about the sugar mountain they once found
in an enchanted cave high on a cliff
which like all miracles could never last.

David Stephenson
Detroit, Michigan

just a few steps more

the trees move in the breeze
little leaves shivering
their roots go down so deep
they do not betray them
I sway unsteady on my feet
our own kind of greeting
a shiver
a sway
a dapple of rain

I missed this bit
the being outside
this is the longest I've been able to stand
I know I'll pay for it later
but right now I bend and creak with the trees
feeling the rain on my skin
instead of just hearing it
I want to stay tasting the cold clarity of late May
but my swaying grows unsteady
this greeting is also goodbye
there's a bed I need to rot in
and I don't want to learn how the cement says hello

Haley Sielinski
Redmond, Washington

Returning to the Village

That gray hut is where I first learned to swim. They pushed us
through a gap in the floorboards. Dropped down a rope
to hold. It took us several panicked kicks to find

that we knew how to do it. Once under, our eyes adjusted
to the salt's burn and gleam. The fish did not care.
They turned their long bodies and became something's dinner.

At home, toweled off, we ate from plates of tasteless
crackers. Bought from the only supermarket, its sides
long-faded to white. The woman who owns it still lives inside.

She has no sons; the fish she sells comes frozen
in boxes from the mainland. I once saw her crouch
on the jetty at dawn and place a basket into the water.

Raise it again full of leathery fish flopping in her arms.
She gutted them. They were so small. I watched
her toss what was left of them back to the ocean.

Stephanie Niu
New York, New York

Saffron Walden

The town is mostly green,
the houses stone or brick,
some with steeply-pitched
brown roofs of thatch
and it is quiet there—
but for certain nights
after the pubs close
when you might hear
the sound a man makes
when he's being kicked,
and next morning early
some woman will be out
sweeping up the broken glass.
It is lovely, really,
well-organized, with flowers
adorning every house.
There is even a village maze
laid out in ancient stones.
Not a bad place to live,
only that nothing ever
happens there, except
in history, which you can
always read about in
some louder place
where there are, perhaps,
far too many people
and too few flowers.

William Heath
Annapolis, Maryland

Ode to the sprig of rosemary

lost in the slit of the oven:
thank you for your aroma
and for the daily reminder
that there is bread in the world

much better than the pre-sliced loaf
that has been shrinking on my counter
over the last two weeks, rather than
succumbing to the staleness of quality.

And to the fairy who stole it
to pad their convection apartment:
I get it. I too steal candles from
under the nose of my roommate.

It is these small sensory joys
so much like ice cubes in the throat
that choke and exhilarate me.
I am late on last month's rent.

Cassady O'Reilly-Hahn
Redlands, California

Moonlight Is an Icy Fanfare

A falling star, wild swings of emotion, doubt and truth, all welling up within, swelling inside, separating from each

other in the shape of tears, covering the corners of their eyes, falling to the floor like falling snow. Someday I won't

wake up alone in the dark, in my bed, my arms weak and empty as the winter snow laying in the fields, waiting to

fall on the cold earth the harvest of my life laid in wait, poised for the shooting star. My lips tremble

but they are calm.

David M. Alper
New York, New York

Kettling

A bird's only story is survival the specialists say,
but the ravens slide down the snowbanks,
then fly back up to reclaim their lost purpose
and slide back down again. Break out
the field guides to identify their types of play.
These will sell well during the domestic epoch,
that year we stayed indoors to avoid the plague.
We tuned up our instruments and sang love songs,
then went out to enjoy the birds, which were
scrambled among the branches calling out
each others' names . . . or so we thought.
So we wanted to believe. We opened up new
franchises of guessing to occupy our minds.
We were caught up in our hypotheticals
like birds in thermals, kettling above the houses
where heat rises in the quiet of our days.
What new heights would result from plumbing
the depths of our souls. We could only conjecture.
That is how we could play with our thinking,
and how too many thoughts could lead us
astray like a bird migrating to the wrong
part of the country, alone, returning again
and again to build another nest that would fail.

Tim Kahl
Elk Grove, California

The Same Is Always Now

In the train stations and subway tunnels death flies above you.
It's the same death on the same wings as it was before
many Springs ago, whether you were Ukrainian or Jew then.

Your feet touch the cold cement where naked bodies are stacked
with missing fingers and limbs because the bombs drop
on the same houses and tear them off, *the same is always now.*

In place of goose-stepping Germans Russians march with legs
extended out of Nazi posters, heads rattling in their helmets;
they are running out of gas and bullets, even Russian bread.

Nearing Passover the current pharaoh sees the Angel of Death
fly above his head, above the road from Moscow to Kyiv
and its geologic scar, Babi Yar, where they burnt the bodies.

The same sirens blare and children fall like silent snow;
for some adults who were children before, it's always then and now:
death comes flying and life ends, always the hardest lesson.

Michael Salcman
Baltimore, Maryland

Red-winged Blackbirds

[Birds] symbolize a degree of freedom that we would nearly give our souls to have....
 —from *How to Know the Birds,* Roger Tory Peterson, Signet Classic, 1949

No one is surprised
when I say I love early spring,
the world still soggy and brown.
But when I say that I love
the red-winged blackbird,
its buzz triumphant from the reeds
it balances upon, its red epaulettes
bright against the drear,
someone always asks *haven't you ever been attacked?*
and doubles down with *they are something fierce.*

When I learn the red-winged blackbird
stakes its territory with a ruthless masculinity—
cultivating harems, impregnating females
with abandon, fending off rivals
by knowing the most songs—
I think of balancing on the marshy edge
of wanting to do what I want
no matter who gets hurt
and writing something beautiful about it.

Jennifer Fandel
Madison, Wisconsin

Solitaire

My grandfather plays solitaire for hours
with a deck black-edged and creased from
years of steady greasing from his fingers until
the cards seem pliable as a slice of cheese.
He sits with a plywood board on his lap,
dealing out stacks, turning them up,
shifting short rows into longer ones, until
there are none, all the while tidying
and re-tidying the cards.
Then starting again.

I am small enough to fit on the arm
of his chair and watch. He hasn't shaved
and has white spikes on his cheeks. He has
a familiar smell of flannel and Lifebuoy soap.
I don't know the game, so just follow the flow
of his hands in their rhythm, the wuffling
sound of the shuffle, the little accordion
of the bridge, the slight *tic* when a card
is laid. I want him to take me to play
in his workshop, crack beech nuts for me,
or tell me a story about being a boy
and rabbit hunting with his uncles.
He keeps playing. Reshuffles.

That is how I remember it—-a restless kid
dropped off on Saturdays at a lonely house
with my grandmother gone. I want him to know
I am there. Though once he made a magic wand
from a dowel and a star cut from balsa wood.
He painted it white and glued on glitter.
So maybe it happened that sometimes
he put his cards down for a moment and
ruffled my hair with a patient hand.
Or maybe I just wished it.

Deborah Pope
Chapel Hill, North Carolina

Sebastian to His Wounds

I love you, little mouths,
portals through which my life passes—
tell them who I am.

Tell the feathered arrows that though they fly
straighter than birds they cannot find
what remains invisible, undying.

Tell the bows that they can bend
like ash trees in a storm or like a crowd
beneath the orator's words,

yet what remains invisible does not bend.
And tell the strings that sing like lyres
when the notched and feathered arrows fly

like startled flocks at the captain's cry,
that the song of the invisible flies
where they cannot.

Tell the archers, guards and friends,
to find themselves in what pours
joyously from your lips.

And tell my friend and benefactor,
the Emperor who holds us all
in his unforgiving hands,

that when we meet on the final day,
invisible no longer,
you will whisper his name and kiss.

Lee Rossi
San Carlos, California

Ode To Dawn & The Coffee Jug

i like how my coffee tastes like loneliness.
the irredeemable kind. i'm poetic enough
to believe the moon sits with me sometimes;
in the saucer; on the desk; the onion layers
of internet tabs; the view leaking across
the patio when the morning is still a yoke
of nightly bodies—two wounded moons
inside my head howling to their eastern cousin
and how quiet is the call? it cannot break the trick
of the coffee, it cannot break the smile slopping
at the wound of the dawn. i'm right there
scrapping at the callus of rest; longing after the fractals
of wholeness beside the lip of my glass jug.

Olumide Manuel
Akure, Ondo State, Nigeria

The Land of Not Enough

attention. Not enough
bandwidth. Not enough
coffee. Not enough
deep sleep. Not enough

evidence. Not enough
fiber. Or food. Not enough
gas. Not enough grace. Not enough
hours in the day. Not enough
information. Not enough

justice. Or jobs. Not enough
kitchen counter space. Not enough
love, or lust. (Or lubrication?) Not enough

money, memory, men. Not enough
natural light. Not enough
oxygen to the brain. Not enough
police. Not enough police reform. Not enough

queered space or quality time. Not enough
reason to leave. Not enough
salt. Not enough serotonin. Not enough
tooth left for a crown. Not enough
understanding. Not enough
vitamin D. Not enough

women in Congress. Not enough
Xanax. Not enough yacht or
yarn to cast off. Maybe enough
zombies.

Paula Reed Nancarrow
Saint Paul, Minnesota

Pomegranate Seeds

I dip the sun in milk
    & leave it out to dry
    next to the papaya—

        bitter,   useful.

What else to do with the migration
        you left in me?

    The salt lick ran dry
        and we are worse for it—animals, again.

Your fingers traced a covenant
    along the corners of my palm

& whole swathes of wisteria
blossomed from my thighs.

    The first thorn drew blood,
        the others touched only scar tissue.

I'd give the crescent back to the moon,

    return the gift of flight,
        coax an ostrich off the ground

        put the pomegranate seeds
            back in place,

if it meant I could forget
    your almond eyes—

    solace in my ruby stained fingertips.

Katey Linskey
Lyle, Washington

Last Day in Kinsale

Lastness isn't a quality we tend to
cultivate, though even Christ said
to be first, be last. To be sure,
to last is an ability admired in things
& often desired. Things are said to
be found in the last place you look,

though a condemned man's last meal is,
at best, a mixed blessing. Last words
get thought out ahead of time
by those for whom words matter.
As last days go, I couldn't have scripted one
more apt for my time in Kinsale, this sky

gray enough ravens confuse gulls for ghosts
of ravens. The well-beaked black birds
fly with lost chums, reminiscing
& feeling blessed. A loon dives
under the Bandon with grace. There is
a world of ideals beneath this one.

George Looney
Erie, Pennsylvania

Among the Dying

Days of rain pool the choked gutter.
A lone crow comes to drink, a beneficiary

of my obsession with the botulism
that troubled Franklin's Arctic expedition—

how first it paralyzed the gaze, then
the muscles of speech, then froze a man

from the extremities upwards. All of us
fear this is how the end will be—

our mind lucid, our body crushed by ice
even as, elsewhere, dogwoods seduce

with plump luster. Come out with me,
I beg my husband, but he eyes the grey sky

and refuses. So it must have been among
Franklin's dying—one dumb robin still

blaring his hopeful song while the rest
knew for a fact they had no chance,

huddling in their own ruin until they lost
even the ragged comfort of their breath.

Devon Balwit
Portland, Oregon

Snow Day

When we were little, brother, we'd spin
in circles in the living room until
we fell down dizzy with laughter,
arms and legs tangled together

in circles in the living room and
outside our window, snow piled up.
Our arms and legs tangled into snowsuits,
boots, wool across our faces, bundled

to run out headlong into snow, piled up
in soft curves. We threw our bodies,
bundled, with wool across our faces
fearless into the cold, sparkling with delight.

Into the soft curves we threw ourselves,
arms and legs spread wide, fearless
in the sparkling cold, deep with delight,
sweeping arcs for angel wings.

Arms and legs spread wide, we
pressed shapes of fearless angels in snow,
sweeping arcs for wings and gowns,
then pulled each other up with mittened hands,

leaving our shapes angels in the snow.
Careful not to trample our prints,
we pulled each other up with mittened hands,
proud of the marks we left behind.

Careful not to trample what we left behind,
when we were little fearless angels,
brother, we pulled each other up.

Joanne Esser
Eagan, Minnesota

Idyll for a Barn Collapsing

A barn in name only now,
it appears to be genuflecting
to the gods of entropy.
The knee of the southwest
corner is a corner no more
as the walls tilt away
from form and all it once kept safe—
goats, foals, stray chickens and
litters of kittens. The mice
long ago ransacked the oats
and corn. What's left inside
are slanted spears of sun
embossed in motes of dust,
and someone's memories.
Behind every fallen barn
stands a dream abandoned.
Earth and time do what they must,
what they've always done—
take back their elements,
one by one.

Frank Coons
Arvada, Colorado

Let It Snow, Let It Snow, Let It Snow

The desert weather—sunny, clear, hot—
goes on day after day, filling some with delight,

but after a time filling others with a flickering
far up behind the eyes, the memory of snow falling

and the grumble and creak in their inmost ear
of an icy blanket sealing over a river.

What lives within such a one is a hunger for cold and cloud,
a persistent memory of crouching at the back

of a cave enfolded in the delight of a chunk
of still warm deer liver held on the tongue,

of its pudding soft texture, its iron tang,
the comfort of its sharp astringency.

Those so afflicted keep both blinds and curtains shut,
pretend they are at a darker, damper, colder latitude

in a time when the edge of the ice was still in reach.
The day, oblivious, burns on.

Joseph Stefani
Tucson, Arizona

Ode to Roadkill

Your first teaching job is an hour commute
one way. Although it's a straight shot of highway,
you didn't expect to pass so much death:

rabbits squished, armadillos with broken backs,
and abandoned dogs chasing tail lights.
Today the sun rises like a blood orange,

like a vigilant fist, and you see, in the distance,
four black blobs lingering around another victim.
Seventy-five miles per hour brings you to a deer.

Her neck is twisted and bent backwards
like a swan, and her hind leg contorts
towards a dry snout. She's a ballet dancer

performing her final scene. Ravens and flies,
buzzing aloof, scurry when you drive by;
how quickly they return in the rearview.

You nearly miss your exit while thinking
about how hard it must be to keep on trucking
after you've been struck by something that refuses to stop,

or how it feels to have your guts
spilled atop the asphalt to the sound of tires
peeling out. You think about how death hangs over you

waiting to swoop down on the side of the road
like curtains closing after dancers take a bow
despite the audience's applause for an encore.

In the parking lot, you hear cars on the highway,
rushing to and from work, or school or home,
someplace where tomorrow is still promised; and you hope,

wherever the destination, that everyone arrives there safely.

Zachary Rea
Springfield, Missouri

Train

When picking fallen coal beside the tracks,
Doc tried to time his chore with the rail
schedules to stand beside a moving train.
Something in their jerk and lurch, the nearness
of each hitch hot with strain, dead weight
heaved against its own resistance.
He could feel the greatness of their bulk,
watch ties sag into gravelbed below each axel,
hear the screech and sheer of side-scraped
wheels, loosened spikes pulsing like pistons
in the ties, the punch of sooty windstrong drafts,
the scent of heated steel above pulverized stone.

Yet sometimes he arrived moments late
and touched the tracks to feel old warmth,
knew even among the evening hush some giant
power had only recently departed and left a tube
of quiet presence where bulk once filled,
like a long exhale into stillness, like a revival
tent after the poles get pulled, a cave mouth
leading out to emerald domes of daylight.

After placing black chunks into his bucket
he listened for the absence of the engine,
vacant as the sky above the empty hall of treeline,
green peepers beginning anew, calling unafraid
as dusk comes on. And if there is a God,
Doc thought, and He somehow got loosed
from the stables of men, perhaps this is how
such a figure would reapproach; with a weighted
stillness, like the silence after a train, a long fabric
of quietude pulled behind a wake of warm rails.

Micah Daniel McCrotty
Piedmont, Tennessee

Situation Comedy

After four episodes of Friends, I sleep.
My podcast says I might be stressed.
I run the dishwasher, after testing

the limit of what I can fit in it,
four pans, two pots, all handles
down. Another limit to understand—

in a dream I stand shovel in hand
over a hole in beach sand. Awake,
I run at seven each morning. I run

to the grocery store, to the bank,
to the gas station, to the bank again.
My podcast guesses I'm depressed.

In the bay of my garage, boxes float,
rowboats in a harbor. A television stand
is a ferry, the spare couch a yacht.

Always one episode of Frasier later,
sleep, dream of a deeper hole, this time
I stand inside to dig. My podcast guesses

I'll listen to a TED Talk about death.
I learn less laundry and more often,
small and smaller cycles. After Seinfeld,

try sleep. Dear Podcast, what will it mean
if the next time I dream of digging, I pile
dirt past my knees, or thighs, or higher?

Ruth Towne
South Berwick, Maine

Barn Swallow

The piled nests, like tree rings,
each year another coil thicker—
    the one above the horse stall,
prodigious, ur-nest, deep as a man's forearm is long—
    one can only imagine
the scene inside: thirty years
    of feather-fluff, chitin and insect wings,
    a mummified hatchling or two—
And still they return, descendants
of the original pair, as simple
    and profound as memory reborn
from scent or sound—a Proustian unfolding of the way
    things used to be and still are and always may be—
their arrival akin to prophecy:
quick flutter, caught from the periphery,
    and there on a cobwebbed beam, a being
    who recognizes what you are and what you do,
    who blesses your labor and your care
    by diving and rising in the air.

Amanda Smith-Hatch
Ontario, New York

Parking Lot Present

for Jane

It's the season of wedging
holidays into crannies of working,
shopping through lunch and in darkness
for the annual torrent of tissue and ribbon.

Extra chairs borrowed for visiting family.
Huge meals gobbled dodging alligators —
layoffs, divorce, unfortunate stock deals —
which bite into conversation when we overdrink.

Which brings me to this moment.
My house overflowing with the people I love most,
I hide in my car, in the library parking lot.
My hands, raw from scouring, unfurl in warm pockets.
Others eye my parking space, but I'm not leaving.
This time to breathe alone is my gift, with love, to me.

Susan Wolbarst
Gualala, California

Synchronicity

She's here when I'm here—
on the bench next to what I
assume is the grave of someone
she knew, loved, possibly hated,
never made amends to—

or, maybe, she just needs some
space, some quiet, after a long day,
and this is the best place to
accommodate that need.

We never speak, not even a nodding
hello; small talk isn't my thing, especially
in the cemetery at dusk. And I don't
want to intrude.

Still, it's a small comfort to know
she's here; our worlds in silent
synchronicity, the day ready to call
it a day. I stall a bit more, take my time
before heading home. Our house gets
too large at night. But you already know this.

Cathy Porter
Omaha, Nebraska

How to Dream in Russian

Tell your husband to turn
off the news, you don't want
to distress your mind before bed.
He mutes the TV but you can still
hear their faces. Donate one hundred dollars
to the humanitarian response in Ukraine
to prove to yourself you're doing
all you can. Check online to see
if Oleg and Yulia, the couple you met
in Bishkek eight years ago
are still alive in Kyiv. They are buying
water and sleeping bags for people running
from the war. Remember, unbidden,
what the military analyst said on the radio
earlier today about how thanks
to Russian chemical weapons, Aleppo
is very peaceful now. Everyone
there is dead. Condemn yourself
for not calling Khalil for the whole pandemic.
Bid yourself remember how well
his kids are doing in Spokane Public Schools
how much they've grown since they stayed
at your house six years ago, bleary-eyed
and bewildered. *Let's eat*
said the middle daughter
when, after only a few days in America
she knew the food was ready.
She put her chin to her chest
and then up to the ceiling
on each word: *Let's. Eat.*
and you ask yourself
if you have ever committed
to anything like she did when
she bid us to the table.
Go to bed but wander
the internet first in search of absolution.
Turn off the light. Wake up to the first
spring sun streaming through the window

knowing, like some women know they are pregnant
before they are told, that you dreamed
in Russian last night. It has not happened
in years. You did not think it would ever
happen again.

Katy Fitzpatrick Shedlock
Spokane, Washington

Jazz

With your father, you play
chess now or other mind
games, debate history
or modern questions. With

me, it's music; we take
turns choosing the songs. Why,
you ask, are the jazz tunes
always about weather:

raindrops or blue skies or
stormy weather or the
sun that always rises,
as it did the summer

of your brother's dying
in a bad sea. The sun's
orange round that slicked the
water as we drove from

the coastal town and the
gulls blowing against the
dawn, and you watching, white
faced, the light filling in.

Becky Kennedy
Jamaica Plain, Massachusetts

CPSIA information can be obtained
at www.ICGtesting.com
Printed in the USA
JSHW061925271222
35433JS00004B/17

9 798985 378047